Ibn al-Haytham

The Man Who Discovered How We See

Peachtree

Libby Romero

NATIONAL GEOGRAPHIC

Washington, D.C.

For Mom and Dad. Thanks. —L.R.

Published by the National Geographic Society, Washington, D.C. 20036.

Trade paperback ISBN: 978-1-4263-2500-7
Reinforced library binding ISBN: 978-1-4263-2501-4
Special sale edition ISBN: 978-1-4263-2616-5

Editor: Shelby Alinsky
Art Director: Callie Broaddus
Editorial: Snapdragon Books
Designer: YAY! Design
Photo Editor: Christina Ascani
Rights Clearance Specialists: Michael Cassady & Mari Robinson
Manufacturing Manager: Rachel Faulise
Producer, 1001 Inventions: Ahmed Salim
Illustrator, 1001 Inventions: Ali Amro

The author and publisher gratefully acknowledge the expert content review of this book led by Professor Mohamed El-Gomati, OBE (University of York) and Professor Salim Al-Hassani (emeritus, University of Manchester) of the Foundation for Science, Technology and Civilisation (United Kingdom), and the literacy review of this book by Mariam Jean Dreher, professor of reading education (University of Maryland, College Park).

The information in this book is based largely on research provided by the exhibit "1001 Inventions and the World of Ibn al-Haytham." The exhibit is a global campaign produced by 1001 Inventions and the King Abdulaziz Center for World Culture in partnership with UNESCO for the International Year of Light 2015. For further information and resources, visit: www.ibnalhaytham.com.

1001 Inventions gratefully acknowledges the support of: Foundation for Science, Technology and Civilisation, Ms. Namira Salim, Shaikh Hisham bin Abdulaziz Al Khalifa, Mr. Naveed Anwar, Kuwait Finance House, Goldfayre Ltd, Almadinah Almunawarah International Academy, Zuhair Fayez Partnership, and those supporters who chose to remain anonymous.

Photo Credits
GI: Getty Images; LOC: Library of Congress; SS: Shutterstock

COVER, Courtesy 1001 Inventions Ltd.; 1 (CTR), nagelestock.com/Alamy; 3 (LORT), SSPL/Science Museum/Art Resource, NY; 5 (CTR), Courtesy 1001 Inventions Ltd.; 6-7 (CTR), Brandon Bourdages/SS; 7 (UP), NG Maps; 8 (CTR), Rue des Archives/PVDE/GI; 9 (UPRT), Courtesy 1001 Inventions Ltd.; 10 (CTR), Buena Vista Images/GI; 10 (LO), Tischenko Irina/SS; 11 (UPLE), Photo Researchers RM/GI; 11 (CTR), SS; 11 (LO), Frank Lukasseck/Corbis; 12-13 (LO), Jon Arnold/JAI/Corbis; 12 (CTR), Courtesy 1001 Inventions Ltd.; 14-15 (UP), Courtesy 1001 Inventions Ltd.; 16 (UPRT), MuslimHeritage.com; 17, Courtesy 1001 Inventions Ltd.; 18-19 (CTR RT), Getty Research Institute; 20-21 (UPRT), Courtesy 1001 Inventions Ltd.; 22-23 (LOLE), Courtesy 1001 Inventions Ltd.; 23 (LE), Wollertz/SS; 24 (CTR RT), Malyugin/SS; 25 (UP), Courtesy 1001 Inventions Ltd.; 27 (CTR), CCI Archives/Science Photo Library; 28 (CTR), *Book of Optics*, Ibn al-Haytham/S.L. Polyak, The Retina/LOC; 29 (CTR), Courtesy 1001 Inventions Ltd.; 30 (LO CTR), Science Source; 31 (UP), The Granger Collection, NYC; 32 (CTR RT), Science Source; 32 (LOLE), Quaoar/SS; 33 (UPRT), Paul Souders/The Image Bank/GI; 33 (CTR LE), Ingram/SS; 33 (CTR RT), arshambo/SS; 33 (LOLE), History of Science Collections/University of Oklahoma Libraries; 35 (UP), Wollertz/SS; 35 (LE), Photo Researchers RM/GI; 35 (RT), Zoonar GmbH/Alamy; 36 (CTR), SS; 37 (CTR), UniqueLight/SS; 38-39 (LO), Terry Eggers/Corbis; 40 (LE), Courtesy 1001 Inventions Ltd.; 41 (CTR), Dudarev Mikhail/SS; 42 (CTR), Bridgeman Images; 42 (LE), Rena Schild/SS; 43 (LE), Bridgeman Images; 43 (RT), The Bridgeman Art Library/GI; 44 (UPRT), Nik Wheeler/Corbis; 44 (CTR LE), Image copyright © The Metropolitan Museum of Art/Image source: Art Resource, NY; 44 (LORT), Bridgeman Images; 45 (UPLE), Janet Kimber/The Image Bank/GI; 45 (CTR RT), *Book of Optics*, Ibn al-Haytham/S.L. Polyak, The Retina/LOC; 45 (CTR LE), GIPhotoStock/Visuals Unlimited, Inc.; 45 (LORT), Bridgeman Images; 46 (UPRT), LOC Prints and Photographs Division; 46 (CTR LE), Brandon Bourdages/SS; 46 (CTR RT), Courtesy 1001 Inventions Ltd.; 46 (LOLE), Photo Researchers RM/GI; 46 (LORT), Courtesy 1001 Inventions Ltd.; 47 (UPLE), CCI Archives/Science Photo Library; 47 (UPRT), Courtesy 1001 Inventions Ltd.; 47 (CTR LE), Anna Azimi/SS; 47 (CTR RT), Zoonar GmbH/Alamy; 47 (LOLE), The Granger Collection, NYC; 47 (LORT), Thinglass/SS; THROUGHOUT (ICON), Shokultd/SS; THROUGHOUT (HEADER), mosaicman/SS

National Geographic supports K–12 educators with ELA Common Core Resources.
Visit natgeoed.org/commoncore for more information.

Printed in the United States of America
15/WOR/1

Table of Contents

Who Was Ibn al-Haytham?

Al-Hasan Ibn al-Haytham (al-HAS-un IB-un al-HAY-thum) was an Arab scholar who lived in the 10th and 11th centuries. He was an expert in science and math. He made important discoveries about light and about the way vision works. He also used a new way to study science that scientists still use today.

Ibn al-Haytham was one of the great thinkers of his time. Since then, his ideas have helped other scientists make new discoveries of their own. Many people think he was one of the most important scientists ever to live.

Centuries

One way to measure time is in centuries. A century is a period of 100 years. For example, the years 1 to 99 = 1st century, 100 to 199 = 2nd century, 200 to 299 = 3rd century, and so on.

This drawing is an artist's idea of what Ibn al-Haytham might have looked like.

Words to Know

SCHOLAR: A person who studies and has much knowledge

Growing Up in the Golden Age

Ibn al-Haytham was born in Basra in C.E. 965, during the Golden Age of Muslim civilization. Little is known about his childhood.

The Golden Age was a time of great learning in the Muslim world, which stretched from southern Spain to China. Men and women of different faiths and cultures studied science from earlier times and other cultures. They wanted to know about the world and to use this knowledge to improve people's lives.

That's a FACT! The calendar we use today begins with the year C.E. 1. The time before that counts backward. It ends in the year 1 B.C.E.

Hagia Sophia in Istanbul

The Golden Age

The Golden Age of Muslim civilization lasted from the 7th to the 13th century. During this time, people made amazing advances in science and created inventions we still use today. They invented early versions of guitars and the first hang glider. They even discovered coffee!

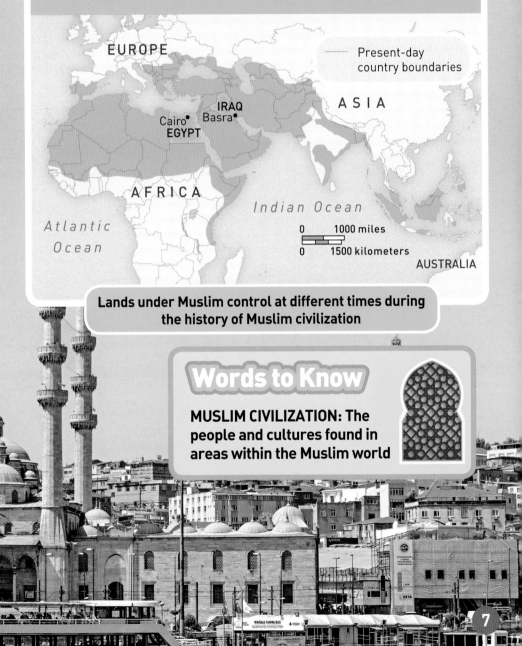

EUROPE

— Present-day country boundaries

ASIA

IRAQ
Cairo• Basra•
EGYPT

AFRICA

Indian Ocean

Atlantic
Ocean

0   1000 miles
0   1500 kilometers

AUSTRALIA

Lands under Muslim control at different times during the history of Muslim civilization

Words to Know

MUSLIM CIVILIZATION: The people and cultures found in areas within the Muslim world

This illustration shows a public library during the Golden Age of Muslim civilization.

This clever clock was made during the Golden Age. It was powered by water and weights. Moving robotic figures told the time.

This was an exciting time for young students like Ibn al-Haytham. Highly trained scholars taught in schools. In Basra, the library held more than 15,000 books. Many of those books were great ancient works that had been translated into Arabic.

Students learned from scholars in many subjects. They talked about discoveries. They discussed and debated ideas. Ibn al-Haytham loved learning about everything and became a great scholar, too. Soon, people far beyond Basra knew about him.

Words to Know

TRANSLATE: To change words from one language into another

In His Time

When Ibn al-Haytham was growing up in Basra in the late 10th century, many things were different from the way they are today.

SCHOOL: Schools were mainly located in mosques (MOSKS), Muslim places of public worship. Both boys and girls started school at age six. Classroom time was very serious, with no laughing or joking allowed.

TRAVEL: People traveled by foot, on horse or camel, and by sea. They made maps and wrote about their travels so that they could share what they learned with others.

HEALTH: Hundreds of years before modern medicine, doctors in the Muslim world could treat all kinds of diseases, fix broken bones, and even do eye operations. They stitched up people after surgery using catgut, a cord made from animal intestines.

TOYS AND GAMES: People liked games that made them think. They played chess and did number puzzles. They built robotic toys that moved and made funny sounds so people could play tricks on one another.

TRADE: Traders traveled in large groups called caravans. They bought and sold goods across three continents.

Trouble in Egypt

Ibn al-Haytham was proud of his knowledge. He was so proud that he claimed he could control the flooding of Egypt's great Nile River by building a dam.

In His Own Words

"If I were given the opportunity, I would implement a solution to regulate the Nile flooding."

His words traveled to Egypt. The caliph (KAY-lif), al-Hakim (al-HA-kim), heard about Ibn al-Haytham's claim. Cairo, the capital of Egypt, is on the banks of the Nile River. The Nile flooded each year, causing great damage to crops. After the flooding, water levels were too low for more crops to grow.

Words to Know

CALIPH: An important Muslim leader, like a president

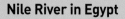

Nile River in Egypt

The caliph invited Ibn al-Haytham to
Cairo and challenged him to control
the flooding. Ibn al-Haytham accepted
the challenge.

He left to explore the Nile. Quickly he saw that he couldn't build a dam that would safely stop the flooding. If any dam could do that, he thought, the master builders of ancient Egypt would have built one long ago.

The Mad Caliph

Although al-Hakim was a great supporter of scholars and scientists, he was also known to be an unreasonable and cruel leader. He ordered many people to be harmed or killed for little or no reason. Because of this, many people called al-Hakim the Mad Caliph.

Ibn al-Haytham returned to Cairo to tell the caliph he had failed. He was afraid. He knew the caliph could be bad-tempered. Instead of punishing him, al-Hakim gave him a job as an expert adviser. But this job was no reward. Being near the caliph put Ibn al-Haytham in danger. To get away from the caliph, Ibn al-Haytham acted like he had gone mad. Al-Hakim put him under house arrest.

Words to Know

HOUSE ARREST: Keeping a person locked in a home as a form of punishment or as a way to protect other people

For more than ten years Ibn al–Haytham was held in Cairo. He could no longer talk with fellow scholars. He could no longer discuss and debate his ideas. He was alone.

But he did have time to think. He had time to read and learn. He had time to come up with new ideas that would change how people saw the world.

A Dazzling Discovery

The Golden Age of Muslim civilization was a time of great discovery. But there were still many things people didn't know. One big question was: How do people see?

For centuries, scholars had debated the ideas of ancient Greek thinkers. Some people believed that rays shoot out of our eyes, making things visible. Others thought that something comes into our eyes, allowing us to see. Ibn al-Haytham wondered if either of these ideas was correct.

This picture illustrates the ancient Greeks' idea that people see because rays shoot out of their eyes.

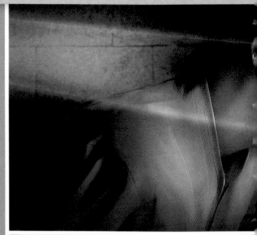

Legend says that
Ibn al-Haytham was
sitting in a dark room
one day. He noticed
a bright light shining
on the wall. He looked
closer. It wasn't just a
beam of light. It was an
image of objects outside
his room. But they were
upside down. How was
any of this possible?

Ibn al-Haytham began to search for
answers. The light was coming through
a tiny hole in the wall. He blocked
the hole with his hand. The image
disappeared. He took his hand away.
The image came back.

Suddenly, he understood. Light bounced off the objects outside, traveled through the hole, and made the image. He thought the opening at the front of an eye must do the same thing. Rays don't shoot out of an eye. Light comes in, just like the light coming in through the hole in the wall! This dark room was like an eye. That's how people see!

The Dark Room

In Ibn al-Haytham's time, many scholars simply believed that ideas from the past were true. They did not question what they read. They didn't think old ideas needed to be tested.

In His Own Words

"If learning the truth is the scientist's goal ... then he must make himself the enemy of all that he reads."

Ibn al-Haytham disagreed. He wanted to test the old ideas, especially those about how people see. He wanted to prove which idea was correct. He also had new evidence from the light in the dark room. So he decided to start testing.

Ibn al-Haytham gathered supplies. He built a small box. A sheet of thin paper made up one side of the box. Across from the paper side was a small hole.

Next, he placed three lit candles outside the box in front of the hole. Then he looked at the sheet of paper.

The Camera Obscura

Ibn al-Haytham's box came to be known as the camera obscura. *Camera* is the Latin word for "room." *Obscura* means "dark." Experimenting with the box, he discovered that a smaller hole created clearer images. This idea led to the modern-day camera.

He saw an upside-down image of the three lit candles. The light from the flames was bouncing off of the candles, traveling through the hole, and making the image. The results were the same as what he had seen in his room. This proved that his idea of how we see was correct.

Light and Vision

Ibn al-Haytham kept testing. He started to have new ideas about light and how we see. Each test showed him new information.

In one test, he observed that the dots of light he saw always lined up perfectly with the beam of light coming in through a pinhole. He concluded that light travels in straight lines.

Words to Know

OBSERVE: To watch carefully as a way to learn something

CONCLUDE: To decide something after careful thought or based on evidence

He also noticed that light coming from different sources never got mixed up as it passed through the pinhole. This gave him more proof that light travels in straight lines. It helped explain why we see exactly what's around us.

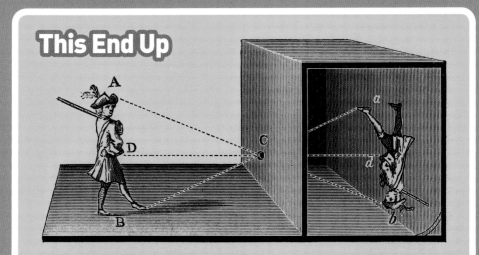

This End Up

Ibn al-Haytham concluded that light travels in straight lines. This diagram shows why objects in the images he saw were upside down. Light bounces off the top part of an object (point A). It travels in a straight line through the hole in the center of the box. The only place the light can land is down low (point *b*). Light travels in straight lines from every part of the object. This flips the whole image upside down. Since Ibn al-Haytham's time, we have learned that this happens in our eyes, too. But our brain knows to flip the image back, and we see the world right side up.

Ibn al-Haytham knew that light coming into the eye was just the first step. More had to happen in order for us to see. He wanted to know what that was. He studied what eyes are made of. He even found and named important parts of the eye.

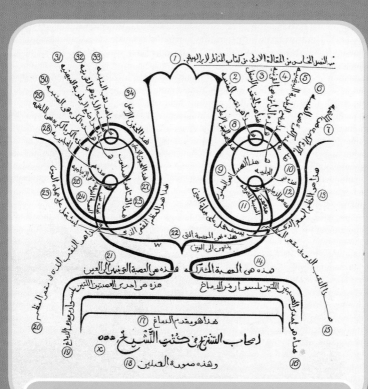

This diagram was based on Ibn al-Haytham's original drawing. It shows not only the parts of the eye but also how eyes are connected to the brain.

Ibn al-Haytham started to write a book about what he learned. In the *Book of Optics*, he explained how he tested his ideas. He wrote down every step of his experiments. He didn't just want to tell people what he had discovered. He wanted people to do the experiments themselves. He wanted them to see why his ideas were right.

This illustration appeared in the Latin edition of the *Book of Optics*, but it was not created by Ibn al-Haytham.

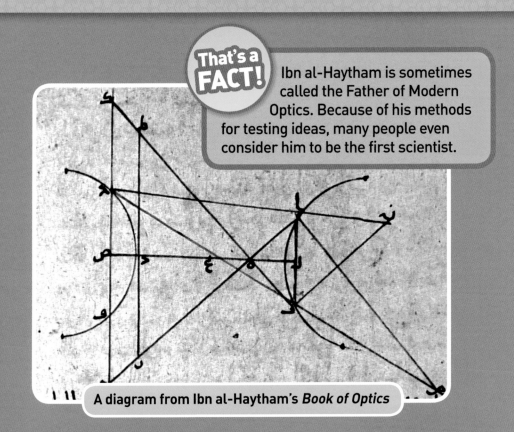

Ibn al-Haytham is sometimes called the Father of Modern Optics. Because of his methods for testing ideas, many people even consider him to be the first scientist.

A diagram from Ibn al-Haytham's *Book of Optics*

The *Book of Optics* encouraged people to ask questions about science. It showed them how to find the answers. It is the first example of the scientific method. Scientists still use this method today.

Words to Know

OPTICS: The science of light and vision

SCIENTIFIC METHOD: A way of using tests and observing the results to answer questions about science

6 COOL FACTS
About
Ibn al-Haytham

Ibn al-Haytham invented a clock powered by water. It may have been the first clock to give time in hours and minutes.

1

Alhazen crater

2

The Alhazen crater on the moon is named after Ibn al-Haytham. So is the asteroid 59239 Alhazen.

Ibn al-Haytham used math to show that moonlight is actually sunlight bouncing off of the moon's surface.

3

4

Ibn al-Haytham's work helped others create modern inventions such as cameras, movie projectors, eyeglasses, microscopes, and telescopes.

Ibn al-Haytham studied things people see that look different from the way they really are. These are called optical illusions. He said they are visual tricks played by the brain.

5

6

Ibn al-Haytham often used math to explain his ideas. The numbers he got weren't always exact, but modern scientists say he was on the right track.

Other New Ideas

Ibn al-Haytham also studied how light moves. He did tests using different types of lenses and mirrors. These tests taught him about reflection. Light reflects, or bounces back, when it hits a surface.

Other experiments with light taught Ibn al-Haytham about refraction. He learned that light refracts, or bends, when it moves through different materials.

Words to Know

REFLECTION: The bouncing back of light from a surface

REFRACTION: The bending of light as it passes through materials

In His Own Words

"Visual objects seen by us through light refraction—across dense material such as water and glass—are bigger than their real size."

Reflection

Refraction

Ibn al–Haytham also watched the sun, the moon, and the stars. This made him ask more questions. He did experiments to find the answers.

He wondered why the sky changes colors as the sun sets. He concluded that rays of sunlight refract as they pass through the air around Earth. When light bends, it separates into different colors.

He wondered why we can't see stars in the daytime. He concluded that the levels of brightness of the daytime sky and the stars are too similar. We see bright objects only when they are next to darker objects, such as the night sky.

He wondered why the moon appears
smaller when it's high in the sky
and larger when it's low in the sky.
He concluded that this is an
optical illusion.

Many scientists have tried to figure out why this happens. Although they have many ideas, no one has been able to find scientific proof. It's one of the oldest unsolved scientific puzzles remaining today.

A Lasting Legacy

Ibn al-Haytham made many important discoveries about light and vision. He did this while he was under house arrest. He continued his work after he was released.

C.E. 965	Around 1010	1010–1021
Born in Basra	Placed under house arrest	Makes important discoveries about light and vision

Ibn al-Haytham's Books

Ibn al-Haytham wrote at least 96 books. Only 55 are still around today. Many of his books are about light. They tell about his studies of the moon, stars, rainbows, mirrors, shadows, and the sun. His most famous book is the *Book of Optics.*

As a free man, he also taught and wrote. Around 1027 he finished the *Book of Optics.* He wrote many other books as well. In 1039, he died in Cairo. He was 74 years old.

1021
Released from house arrest

Around 1027
Finishes the *Book of Optics*

1039
Dies in Cairo at age 74

For a time, Ibn al-Haytham's work seemed to be forgotten. Then in the early 12th century, his books were translated into Latin. Because more people knew Latin than Arabic, more scientists and scholars could study his work.

NAME: Roger Bacon
LIVED: 1220–1292
STUDIED: Bacon used the scientific method to study light. He told other scientists to test their ideas and observe the results, too.

NAME: Kamal al-Din al-Farisi
LIVED: 1267–1319
STUDIED: Al-Farisi studied Ibn al-Haytham's work on refraction. He then did tests with glass jars full of water to find out how rainbows are made.

Over the centuries, many great thinkers learned from Ibn al-Haytham, just as he learned from ancient scholars who came before him.

QUIZ WHIZ

See how many questions you can get right!
Answers are at the bottom of page 45.

1

Where was Ibn al-Haytham born?

A. Greece
B. Cairo
C. Basra
D. Egypt

2

Ibn al-Haytham lived during the _____ of Muslim civilization.

A. Bronze Age
B. Silver Age
C. Iron Age
D. Golden Age

What does *camera obscura* mean?

A. Photograph
B. Dark room
C. Light ray
D. Pinhole

3

4

Ibn al-Haytham claimed he could control the _____ of the Nile River.

A. flowing
B. flooding
C. drying up
D. saltiness

What did Ibn al-Haytham study while under house arrest?

5

A. Light and vision
B. Hearing and sound
C. Smell and odor
D. Touch and feel

6

Ibn al-Haytham learned that light travels in _____.

A. refraction
B. straight lines
C. reflection
D. optical illusions

Who came up with new ideas by studying Ibn al-Haytham's work?

7

A. Kamal al-Din al-Farisi
B. Johannes Kepler
C. Isaac Newton
D. All of the above

Glossary

CALIPH: An important Muslim leader, like a president

MUSLIM CIVILIZATION: The people and cultures found in areas within the Muslim world

OBSERVE: To watch carefully as a way to learn something

REFRACTION: The bending of light as it passes through materials

SCHOLAR: A person who studies and has much knowledge

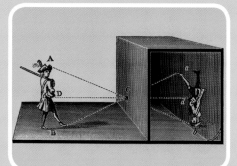

CONCLUDE: To decide something after careful thought or based on evidence

HOUSE ARREST: Keeping a person locked in a home as a form of punishment or as a way to protect other people

OPTICS: The science of light and vision

REFLECTION: The bouncing back of light from a surface

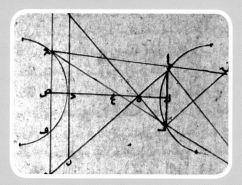

SCIENTIFIC METHOD: A way of using tests and observing the results to answer questions about science

TRANSLATE: To change words from one language into another

Index

NOTE: While best efforts have been used in preparing this book, the publishers and contributors recognize that some parts of this book may be disputed and the subject of continued research. This book contains a number of fictionalized images that attempt to depict part of the life of Ibn al-Haytham that may or may not be completely accurate.